Meditation

Published by Hinkler Pty Ltd
45–55 Fairchild Street
Heatherton Victoria 3202 Australia
www.hinkler.com

hinkler

Book packager: Tall Tree Ltd
Author: Venerable Thubten Lhundrup
Additional content: Nicola Hodgson
Packaging and cover design and illustration: Rachael Jorgensen

Images © Hinkler Pty Ltd or Shutterstock.com

ISBN: 978 1 4889 4556 4

Printed and bound in China

ELEVATE

Meditation

Venerable Thubten Lhundrup

hinkler

CONTENTS

" Meditate … do not delay,
lest you later regret it. "

Buddha

What is meditation?

In our lives today we are often so busy that we don't have time to stop and take stock of our inner feelings and thoughts. Meditation is a useful way of calming the mind and it can have huge benefits to the rest of our lives. Meditation is a way of checking in with our emotions and finding a way to better understand them.

It doesn't have to mean sitting down cross legged in silence for many hours at time. It can be fitted into our everyday lives and become a habit that will change your perspective on life. It is a skill that can be learned and with patience and practise will become easier over time. Meditation is a way of training your mind away from the everyday distractions and using breathing to focus on the present moment.

"

It is indeed a radical act of love just to sit down and be quiet for a time by yourself.

"

Jon Kabat-Zinn

Benefits of meditation

Regular meditation practice has many benefits. Meditation can help reduce stress levels and can help lower blood pressure and regulate your heart rate and breathing. It can improve the quality of sleep, increase your energy levels and help you deal with whatever life throws at you.

Many religions find spiritual benefits from meditation. In the Buddhist belief system meditation helps you familiarise your mind with beneficial states and thoughts – thoughts such as assisting others, compassion, treating others equally and morality. You begin to realise that non-virtuous thoughts such as hatred, anger, greed and jealousy are destructive not only to the people you direct them at but also to yourself.

Meditation in the form of prayer is a part of other religions including Islam, Christianity and Judaism. It is also important within Hinduism, where the practice of yoga is linked to a meditative state called *dhyana*.

The monkey mind

The most common experience for someone meditating for the first time is the realisation of how busy the mind is. It is not until we attempt to quieten the mind that we realise there is a continuous arising of thoughts, memories, sounds, physical sensations and visions. By understanding the current nature of your mind, you can begin to learn how to change it.

This is what the Lamas (Buddhist teachers or gurus) call the 'monkey-mind'. Just like a monkey's mind, ours too is continually jumping from one object to the next. By understanding the current nature of your mind, you can begin to learn how to change it.

The success of meditation depends on many factors, including your state of mind before you begin, your stress level and physical tiredness. As a result, some sessions are better than others. Don't expect too much, especially to begin with. Even experienced meditators have bad days. Be patient. Be gentle on yourself.

> ## Meditation is not about stopping thoughts, but recognizing that we are more than our thoughts and our feelings.

Arianna Huffington

When, where and how

The meditation environment

For a beginner, regular and brief meditation sessions are more beneficial than occasional attempts at longer sessions. If we try to do too much too soon there is the chance of becoming disheartened, feeling that meditation is just a painful, frustrating experience.

How often should I meditate?

For a beginner, regular and brief meditation sessions are more beneficial than occasional attempts at longer sessions. If we try to do too much too soon there is the chance of becoming disheartened, feeling that meditation is just a painful, frustrating experience.

Posture

The following seven points help the subtle energies in the body flow freely. They are not compulsory, though. The main concern is to be comfortable enough to avoid moving around but not so relaxed that you fall asleep or experience dullness.

1. Cross your legs if sitting on the ground or on a cushion. Sitting on a chair is also fine.
2. Place your hands palms facing upwards on your knees and hold your thumb and index fingers together in a circle shape. If you don't feel comfortable like this hold your palms facing upwards, place your right hand on top of your left with the tips of your thumbs gently touching, hands resting in your lap.
3. Hold your back comfortably straight: not so rigid that you experience discomfort or tension during the session.
4. Relax your jaw and allow your tongue to rest behind your front, top teeth.
5. Tilt your head slightly forward.
6. Your eyes may be closed, although this can increase the chance of falling asleep. If you have your eyes open, have them only slightly open, gazing downwards without focusing.
7. Hold your shoulders level and keep your elbows slightly away from your body.

66

The quieter you become,
the more you are able to hear.

99

Rumi

Be patient

As a patient mother will gently bring a curious, crawling baby back on to the blanket, we should be the same with our mind when it wanders. Patiently and gently bring it back to the breath, understanding that wandering or distraction is part of its current nature.

Relax

While effort is important, it is possible to try too hard to meditate. Meditation should be an enjoyable, inspiring experience. Ideally, you should be looking forward to the next meditation session and not feeling that it is a chore, finding reasons to avoid it.

If you find yourself becoming frustrated at an apparent lack of success, it may be best to take a break. Go for a walk. Get some fresh air. Try again later in the day.

"

Your goal is not to battle with the mind, but to witness the mind.

"

Swami Muktananda

"

Meditation is not about feeling a certain way. It's about feeling the way you feel.

"

Dan Harris

Meditation and the mind

We are inclined to talk about our mind as something solid like a container or maybe even a filing cabinet located in our head. We often say such things as: 'I'll keep it in mind', 'My mind is full of thoughts', etc. However, the mind is not a physical object. No matter how skilful a surgeon may be, they are unable to extract the mind from a body and hold it in their hands.

Many of the practices associated with meditation come from Buddhism. Buddha's teachings tell us that the mind is formless: a beginningless, endless, dynamic process of experiences that are continually arising. From beginningless time, our minds have been reincarnating and experiencing the various sufferings of a *samsaric* (from *samsara*, the cycle of death and rebirth) existence. Our bodies, in different states of existence, act like vehicles for the mind.

As long as we are satisfied with this sort of existence and do nothing, it will continue. But by becoming aware of the nature and potential of our mind, we can begin to understand that profound changes are possible.

Karma

The experiences that are currently arising and forming our mind are not doing so without cause. For something to exist or come into existence there must be a reason: a cause or action to create the effect. These experiences are driven by karma, the Law of Cause and Effect. Our mind is a result of our past actions causing effects to arise now.

Creating causes for happiness

If we are able to modify our behaviour appropriately, understanding that certain actions bring certain results, then we can begin to create the causes for happiness in the future instead of suffering. To start, we need to develop an understanding of the nature of our mind: then we will have an informed idea of what changes to make.

A more peaceful mind, contentment, less worry, less stress and deeper happiness: all this is possible, as well as a more profound love and appreciation for those close to us and for all sentient beings. A mind that looks at other sentient beings with compassion, love and care is one that will convert all our actions into a cause to attain an enlightened mind. With this sort of mind, our resulting actions will create happiness, not only for us but also for those we come into contact with.

Understanding negative actions

If the reverse is true, then it is easy to see what the result would be – negative actions creating unhappiness and disharmony in our minds and in the minds of those we come into contact with. It is essential to be aware of our actions and understand their consequences.

The priceless and very precious positive state of mind is our responsibility to cultivate and maintain, as there are few sources of assistance from outside. The positive influences in our lives are greatly outnumbered by negative influences! In any given day, our minds are exposed to an overwhelming amount of information via radio, television, newspapers, magazines, billboards and, of course, other people. Most of this information is not a positive influence for our minds. We need to be more discriminating with the input our minds receive, to minimise the harmful effects that are accumulated so easily.

Cultivating positive thoughts

The first step in cultivating a positive state of mind is awareness. The next step is having the willingness and motivation to investigate, analyse and identify positive or negative, constructive or destructive influences and states of mind. This is not an easy process. It takes great effort to be diligent and maintain a virtuous mind.

It is said that it is not possible for a negative thought to be in our mind at the same time as a positive thought. Considering this, we need to consciously cultivate the positive thoughts and swamp the negative ones, outnumber them, rather than fighting them and getting frustrated when they dominate.

With the practice of meditation, we can familiarise our mind with appropriate thoughts. With practice, meditation and a mind of compassion for others, we are doing more than just wishing peace, happiness and good conditions for others – we are also counteracting our own hatred, anger and negative states of mind.

66

To understand the immeasurable, the mind must be extraordinarily quiet, still.

99

Jiddu Krishnamurti

Nowhere can man find a quieter
or more untroubled retreat than
in his own soul.

Marcus Aurelius

Meditation, ethics and wisdom

In meditation, it is possible to transform mere intellectual or academic knowledge into a deep and profound understanding related to one's own experience.

To attain these states and then clean the 'mirror' of the mind, we need to also practise morality to lead an ethical life. By doing so, we are more able to destroy the habits of greed, ignorance and hatred.

Wisdom is gained by hearing, learning, contemplating and thinking, but most importantly by meditating. Through meditation we overcome the ignorance or incorrect perception of our self and of all phenomena.

Observing ethics or morality stops negative actions that, due to the certainty of karma, will result in more suffering – actions of body, speech and mind that are harmful not only to us but others as well. Wisdom is not possible without meditation and effective meditation is not possible without ethics.

> Learn to be calm and you will always be happy.

Paramahansa Yogananda

What is mindfulness?

Our mind can be our own greatest enemy! If control can be gained over the mind, then control will be gained over everything. Meditation in which we watch the breath is intended to develop mindfulness.

Mindfulness is the ability of the mind to maintain attention on an object. This ability is crucial in advanced levels of meditation, where undistracted focus on an object for great lengths of time is necessary. Mindfulness in our everyday activities also benefits us immediately by contributing to a peaceful, stress-free mind.

From the moment we wake in the morning, we tend to follow the impulses of the 'monkey-mind', with occasional periods of taking control to focus on the task at hand. As a result, many actions are carried out subconsciously and we are unable to recall doing them.

You may have had the experience of driving to a destination, arriving, and then not being able to recall how you got there. While we may have times where we are focused on a task, more often than not, we are thinking of other things.

Think of a recent face-to-face conversation you had with someone. What thoughts were going through your mind at the time? Were you really listening to the other person, or were you just hearing part of what they said while busily thinking of other things?

Practising mindfulness

Much of the time we are not really listening. We half hear, then quickly make assumptions about what the person is saying and start to think of appropriate responses. It is not often that we really listen mindfully.

When we are physically ill, we may be distracted by pain or discomfort, resulting in an inability to carry out physical actions properly. So it is with our mind. Distracted by other thoughts, we are unable to concentrate on the task at hand. This can result in not doing tasks to the best of our ability. We may be doing the task to simply get it over and done with rather than doing it mindfully.

By practising mindfulness, we can become discerning about the thoughts we let into our mind. More importantly, we can check our motivation for carrying out an action. What are the consequences of the action? Is it an action that will create happiness or suffering for others and myself? Is the action motivated by the thought of cherishing myself at the expense of others? Is there a more skilful way to handle this situation?

If we can develop mindfulness, we begin to take control of our mind rather than be controlled by it. Less stress, improved concentration and a feeling of more control over our lives are all possible if we make the effort!

"

A most useful approach
to meditation practice is to
consider it the most important
activity of each day. Schedule
it as you would an extremely
important appointment,
and unfailingly keep your
appointment with the infinite.

"

Roy Eugene Davis

Hand positions

When meditating you may wonder what you should do with your hands. You can hold them in any relaxed position you find comfortable but there are a few traditional Buddhist and Hindu positions called *mudras* that you could try until you find what feels natural to you:

Gyan Mudra: used for relaxation and to help you keep your mind focused during meditation. Circle your index fingers on both hands round to meet your thumbs.

Dhyana Mudra: place your two hands in your lap with the right hand resting gently on top of the left hand with fingers fully stretched and the two thumbs touching each other. The hands and fingers form a triangle shape, which is symbolic of spiritual fire and the palms form an empty bowl ready to receive knowledge and wisdom.

Shuni Mudra: also known as the 'seal of patience', this mudra is helpful for cultivating patience. Circle your middle finger on each hand round to connect with your thumb.

Patience pays. Wait. Let the hand of God work for you. The One who has created you, let Him create all the environments, circumstances, and facilities and faculties.

Yogi Bhajan

Breath meditation

Let's try a simple meditation now. By placing your thought on the breath, it is possible to quieten a busy mind and improve concentration.

The aim is to become aware of the breath as it enters and leaves your body by concentrating on the rise and fall of the abdomen or the sensation of the breath passing through your lips or nostrils.

With the exhalation of each breath, count one, two, three, etc. Set yourself an achievable target of say seven to begin with. When sensations of quietness, stillness and peace eventually occur, hold them as best you can and experience them as fully as possible. When you are distracted or lose that sensation, return to the breath.

Distractions

Distractions come in many forms. Sounds, visions, physical sensations such as pain in the knees or an itch, happy or unhappy memories, memories of people and events that you have not thought about for ages may come up during your practice.

If you find that you are distracted easily, do not get angry or frustrated. This is the nature of the 'monkey-mind' and an awareness of this nature is actually a sign of progress. The best way to handle these distractions is to not indulge them or attempt to repel them. As they arise in your mind, they will also disappear of their own accord. Simply acknowledge them and return the thought to the breath and resume counting.

"

Learn to be calm and you
will always be happy.

Paramahansa Yogananda

Walking meditation

Walking meditation is a wonderful complement to seated meditation, and is particularly helpful if you find it difficult to focus while sitting, or at times when you're experiencing strong emotion. A natural outdoor location where you won't be disturbed – such as a safe, quiet park – is ideal.

When you walk try to find somewhere that you're familiar with. This way, you won't be distracted from your meditation in thinking about which way to go or thinking about what you're seeing as you walk along. You may choose to walk along a footpath or around a park that you know very well that is close to your home. Try walking along one way and then back again along the same path. Some parks even have walking labyrinths laid out on the ground for meditation and to aid focus.

Focus your attention on your breathing as you walk and on carefully placing your feet on the ground in a mindful way. When you begin this practice you might only feel comfortable walking in this way for a short time, perhaps 5 or ten minutes. Gradually build up the time spent in your meditation to a length that feels comfortable to you.

A walking meditation can bring about a number of benefits including improved mood, better concentration, an awareness of your body and mind and a feeling of a connection between you and the place where you walk.

Begin the walking meditation by standing still with your weight distributed evenly on both legs. Let your arms and hands fall by your sides and hold your back comfortably straight, just as in seated meditation.

Close your eyes, and begin with a short breath meditation to focus your attention. Then, open your eyes and begin walking slowly.

Note your surroundings lightly, and observe the sensations that arise as your body moves: the touch of each foot to the ground, the feeling of your clothing shifting, the brush of the air on your skin.

Walk as if you are kissing the Earth with your feet.

Thich Nhat Hanh

"

If you are facing the right
direction, all you need to
do is keep on walking.

"

The Buddha

Gazing meditation

Gazing meditation, or *trataka* in Sanskrit, is a powerful method of focusing the mind by engaging our most dominant sense – sight. In *trataka*, we gaze at a small object. A candle flame is the most common item, but other good choices are a single flower, a mandala or picture of significance to you, or even the rising moon.

When you do this mindful meditation you should not concentrate on the object, but use it as a focus of your awareness. If you find your focus and your gaze shifting away from the object, gently bring it back to the object and continue.

It is believed that this practice can have a number of positive benefits including increased levels of clarity and concentration, reduced stress. It also builds willpower and can help with the symptoms of anxiety and depression. You may also feel gratitude as you focus on an object you may have seen many times before as you notice the details and beauty of the object. This could even be something as simple as a wooden spoon or bowl you have in your kitchen that you use every day.

Before you begin the gazing meditation, place your object at least an arm's length away and just below eye level. You may need a small table, stool or shelf to achieve this. If using a candle, close the doors and windows to prevent draughts before lighting it and sitting down.

Begin with a minute or two of breath meditation. Then, open your eyes if they are closed and gaze steadily at your meditation object. Try not to blink; keep your eyes and face as relaxed and quiet as possible.

When your eyes begin to water or become sore, close them and visualise the flame or object at your third eye, between your eyebrows. When that image begins to fade, open your eyes again and repeat the process of gazing at the object.

To protect your eyes, limit gazing meditation to no more than ten minutes, particularly if you use a candle flame, and do not practise it daily.

If the mind falls asleep, awaken it. Then if it starts wandering, make it quiet. If you reach the state where there is neither sleep nor movement of mind, stay still in that, the natural (real) state.

Ramana Maharshi

Eating meditation

Eating mindfully can transform how you think about and relate to your body and to food, and can bring awareness to how you eat. First try this type of meditation with a small piece of food, such as a piece of fruit or vegetable. Then, as you become more familiar with it, try a more substantial dish or a meal. Sit at a table with your food in front of you, making sure you're comfortable, able to relax and won't be disturbed.

If you eat mindfully, you will become more aware of what you're eating and how much you're eating. Too often we eat without really thinking about it. You may be working and grab something to eat at your desk or eat your breakfast on the way to a meeting. If you stop and think by following the meditation on the next page, you'll enjoy your meals more and you'll likely eat less and feel the health benefits that result from that. Many people also make healthier choices if they eat mindfully as they stop themselves from choosing foods that are quick and easy but not necessarily the healthiest choices.

"

Meditation is choosing not to engage in the drama of the mind but elevating the mind to its highest potential.

"

Amit Ray

Before you eat, take several deep breaths to centre yourself. Focus on your body, your feelings and your appetite.

Next, smell the food, letting its aroma wash over you and noting its effect on you. Look at the food and think about what contributed to its creation and how it made its way to you – the sun, the rain, the earth, the animals, the people involved. Pause to feel grateful for the blessing of food.

Now, take your first bite and chew slowly and with purpose. Focus completely on the feeling of the textures and the shape of the food in your mouth, and then on the intensity of the flavours and the sensations of the tastes spreading through your mouth. Chew the food thoroughly, being aware of what your tongue and your teeth are doing.

Finally, swallow the food, listening to your body's response to the nourishment and how it affects your hunger and appetite. If your mind wanders, work on pulling your attention back to your body and the food. Repeat until your food is finished, then take several deep breaths, enjoying the sensation of well-being.

Compassion meditation

Also known as a metta or loving-kindness meditation, a compassion meditation helps you develop compassion, care, warmth and love towards both others and yourself. Several phrases stating your intention to practise compassion are silently repeated, first directed inwards to yourself and then outwards towards a person or persons upon whom you wish to focus. Make sure you are sitting or lying somewhere that is quiet and comfortable before you start.

Close your eyes and take several deep breaths. Focusing inwards and create an image of yourself in your mind, then slowly and gently repeat to yourself, 'May I be happy. May I be well. May I be free of pain and sorrow. May I be at peace.' Repeat this several times, over and over. You can choose other similar phrases if you prefer.

Next, focus on someone else. They can be a friend, a family member, a colleague – it's up to you. Again, create an image of them in your mind, then repeat to yourself, 'May you be happy. May you be well. May you be free of pain and sorrow. May you be at peace.'

You can adjust the phrases to suit their circumstances and your feelings towards them if you wish. Refocus the meditation on other people in your life, finishing when it suits you.

"

Remember the blue sky.
It may at times be obscured by
clouds, but it is always there.

"

Andy Puddicombe

Sound meditation

Sound has been used as part of meditation for thousands of years. Using sound can help deepen the meditation, expand the consciousness and focus the mind.

There are many ways you can incorporate sound into a meditation: some versions use tradition instruments such as Tibetan gongs and singing bowls, didgeridoos or shamanic drums; some focus on vocal sounds and chanting; and others draw the meditator's attention to the everyday sounds going on around them as they practice.

This type of meditation can be especially beneficial when done in a group, as the energy of the other participants can heighten and magnify the experience. However, sound is also extremely useful for a meditation in a private session or a solo meditation using recorded sounds, which can be easily found online.

Lie down and close your eyes or if you are using a gong to make your own sound remain seated in a comfortable position. Take several deep breaths to centre yourself before commencing the sound meditation.

When your chosen sound starts, focus your attention on it. Feel how it reverberates through you and around you. Listen to the sound in its entirety, following it from its beginning to its end. Note any fluctuations in tone, pitch or volume, but do not attach any meaning to those changes – simply be mindfully at one with the sound as it is at each moment.

Try not to anticipate any changes or pre-empt where you think the sound might go: your focus should be completely on the present. Focus on ensuring your breathing stays constant throughout the meditation as the waves of sound wash over you, even if the tempo of the sound changes or if there are any silences or pauses.

Attachment meditation

In this meditation, you relive your day so far. Possibly the first action of your day had to do with staying in bed for just five more minutes or the desire to get to the kitchen for breakfast. Maybe there was a disturbing thought of things that had to be done at work or a pleasant thought of having lunch with a friend.

What other thoughts and actions occurred as the day progressed? Impatience or even anger when you had to wait in a queue at the bank? Satisfaction when you drove into the last parking space before someone else? Downhearted when you realised you had to spend the day with someone you did not like? Delighted when your boss praised you in front of others?

If we're honest with ourselves, we'll see that our day is filled with thoughts and actions that are directed at avoiding suffering in its many forms and experiencing happiness. This is a motivation common to all: the wish to experience happiness and avoid suffering.

There is, of course, no problem with possessions, wealth, a comfortable lifestyle. The real problem is in the mind, with the underlying belief that these things will make us truly happy forever.

Begin with a few minutes of breath meditation as described earlier. As best you can, relive the day so far – from the moment you woke up to the present. Consider each action you carried out: not just the big, more significant actions but all the smaller ones as well.

Then think of a previous object of desire you obtained: a relationship or even a situation. If at the time we knew what we know now – that they were impermanent and had no chance of living up to our expectations – would we have suffered so much to obtain them? Would we have placed such importance on them? Would we have become so overwhelmed by the thought of having to have them or having to avoid them otherwise our life would be ruined?

Finish the meditation by considering ways in which you may be able to understand the impermanent nature of phenomena in your life. Appreciating them in a more rational way can prevent the extremes of attachment and desire or aversion and anger.

Consider the peace and contentment that this would create in your mind.

> **When meditation is mastered, the mind is unwavering like the flame of a candle in a windless place.**
>
> Bhagavad Gita

Body scan meditation

A body scan meditation is one where you focus on each part of the body in turn, noticing how it feels before moving on to the next part. Read through the text below and then try to carry out the meditation with your eyes closed. At each point during the meditation, don't try to change the way you feel, just observe and notice how you feel.

Begin by making yourself comfortable. You can sit in a chair with your back straight or sit on a cushion on the floor, or even lie down, whatever feels comfortable for you.

Begin to breathe deeply and slow your breath. Breathe in through your nose and out through your nose or mouth. Feel your stomach expand on an inhale and relax and let go as you exhale.

Begin to let go of noises around you. Begin to shift your attention from outside to inside yourself. If you are distracted by sounds in the room, simply notice this and bring your focus back to your breathing.

Now slowly bring your attention down to your feet. Begin observing sensations in your feet. You might want to wiggle your toes a little, feeling your toes against your socks or shoes. Just notice, without judgment. Just allow yourself to feel the sensation of not feeling anything.

Next, focus on your legs, from the ankles and calves up to the knees and thighs. Observe the sensations you are experiencing throughout your legs. If your mind begins to wander during this exercise, gently notice this without judgment and bring your mind back to the part of your body you are working with.

Bring your attention to your mid back and upper back. Allow the tension to leave your body as you breathe out. Move on to focus to your stomach and the parts of your body internally in this area.

Focus your awareness on the chest and heart and notice your heartbeat. Observe how the chest rises during the inhale and how the chest falls during the exhale. As you breath out, bring the focus to your hands and fingertips.

Next, bring your awareness up into your arms. Exhale, and feel the tensions in this area soften and release. Concentrating on the breath and shift your focus to the neck, shoulder and throat. As you breathe, allow the tension to leave this part of your body.

Slowly begin to move your attention to the scalp, head and face. Notice how this part of your body feels. Exhale, and let the tension leave this area.

Finally, slowly let your focus move to cover your whole body from the top of your head down to bottom of your feet and toes. Keep breathing deeply and evenly in through the nose and out through your mouth.

Let your attention to expand out to include the entire body as a whole. Bring into your awareness the top of your head down to the bottom of your toes. Feel the gentle rhythm of the breath as it moves through the body.

As you come to the end of this practice, take a full, deep breath, taking in all the energy of this practice. Exhale fully. And when you are ready, open your eyes and return your attention to the present moment. As you become fully alert and awake, consider setting the intention that this practice of building awareness will benefit everyone you come in contact with today.

Emotion meditation

Using some of the skills you have learned earlier in this book you can do this meditation, which is designed to help you make sense of the emotions you are feeling, whether those are good or bad. The aim is to notice what you're feeling and to accept those feelings.

If you become adept at this practice it will help you face the feelings that inevitably arise on a daily basis. You'll be able to see that they are not permanent and that they will pass. This practice will also help you to uncover feelings that you've hidden below the surface. There may be issues that you're aware of but that you find difficult to face, so you distract yourself by looking at your phone or by eating mindlessly. However, if you can look at these emotions and feelings directly and acknowledge them you will feel less stress and experience these feelings less intensely.

Over time and with practice this form of meditation can help you manage your stress levels, so when you're faced with a difficult situation that makes you feel angry or stressed you are able to recognize those feelings and become detached, able to reach a state of self-acceptance. You will also be able to recognize when you're in a calm and relaxed state emotionally and take pleasure from that feeling. Another benefit of emotional meditation can be that you are able to let go of underlying negative feelings and feel lighter and more open to new opportunities and experiences.

Begin by making yourself comfortable. You can sit in a chair with your back straight or sit on a cushion on the floor, or even lie down, whatever feels comfortable for you.

You may either keep your eyes open and unfocused without looking at anything in particular or gently close them and look downwards. Focus on the breath, breathing gently in through the nose and out through the mouth several times.

Begin to take notice of how you are feeling right now. Don't think about those emotions too deeply, just notice them and acknowledge how your feel, whether that is happy, sad, angry, joyful or anxious. If you feel your focus shifting, bring it back to your breath and release any tension in your body.

After ten minutes gradually bring your attention back to your surroundings and away from your inner feelings. Think about the emotions, thoughts and feelings that you uncovered and make notes in your meditation journal (see page 94).

Chakras

The seven chakras are the main energy centres in the body. The work 'chakra' is Sanskrit for 'wheel' and when those wheels or energy points are open, energy can run through your body and harmony exists between body and mind. Knowledge of chakras has been around for centuries and stems from ancient Hindu teachings.

The chakras are aligned in the human body from the top of the head and then down through the midline of the body. Energy enters these points from the front and the back of the body. At times, these points can become blocked or imbalanced, which can have an effect on the way we feel emotionally and physically. Meditation can be used to help us unblock the chakras and restore balance so that we can operate at our optimum level of physical, emotional and spiritual wellbeing. There are other minor chakras in the hands and feet which can also be activated through meditation and yoga exercises.

The seven major chakras

Chakra	Location	Sanskrit name	Represented by
Base chakra	Base of the spine	Muladhara	A lotus of four petals
Sacral chakra	Lower abdomen	Svadhisthana	A lotus of six petals
Solar plexus	Solar plexus	Manipura	A lotus of 10 petals
Heart chakra	Middle of the chest	Anahata	A lotus of 12 petals
Throat chakra	At the throat	Visuddha	A lotus of 16 petals
Third eye	At the third eye	Ajna	A lotus of two petals
Crown chakra	Top of the head	Sahasrara	A lotus of 1000 petals

Chakra meditation

Begin by finding a quiet place where you will not be disturbed. Sit in a position that feels comfortable to you, either sitting on a chair with a straight back or with your legs crossed on a meditation cushion. You might place your hands gently on your knees with your palms facing up. Cast your eyes downward without focussing on a particular object, or close them gently.

Take a deep breath, allowing your belly to expand outward as you breath in through your nose. Count to four slowly until your lungs are completely full of air. Hold the air lightly in your lungs for another count of four and then exhale the air out of your mouth to a count of four.

When the air is out of your lungs, hold for a final count of four. Repeat this twice more before you return to a regular breathing pattern.

Picture the chakra at the base of your spine (the root chakra). Spend at least one minute picturing it as a spinning red wheel or a red lotus flower with glowing petals. Imagine it gaining energy and spinning with more and more ferocity.

Allow that chakra to continue growing with energy, then move on to the next chakra – the sacral chakra – and repeat.

Work your way up your body, bringing your attention to each chakra in turn, until you reach the crown chakra.

Imagine all your chakras spinning and humming with energy for several moments. Breath in for four, hold for four and release for four, as described above. Repeat twice more then gradually bring your focus back to your surroundings. Take some time to record your feelings in your meditation journal.

66

The mind is definitely something
that can be transformed, and
meditation is a means
to transform it.

99

Dalai Lama

Yoga and meditation

A regular yoga practice and meditation work together to promote reduced stress and increased good health and well-being. Many yoga poses and stretches will help you to meditate more effectively as they will increase your ability to sit and focus on your breath, which is a part of some many meditation traditions. There are many yogic meditations online or look for a class near you to find out more.

One of the best-known yoga sequences that can become a form of meditation is the Sun Salutation or Surya Namaskar, which is a series of movements that flow one into another. When you do these movements in conjunction with conjunction with the breath this can become a form of meditation as you focus on your breath and movement at the same time as bringing your mind and body together.

If you are new to yoga try a mountain pose (tadasana). Stand with your feet hip width apart and let your arms fall down by your sides with your palms turned out. Close your eyes or gaze downwards without focusing on anything in particular. Take a deep breath in through your nose then release all the air through your mouth. Repeat this slowly and gently. Let the tension leave your body. Try to remain in this position for five minutes, slowly breathing in and out.

Yogic breathing

When you're doing the Sun Salutation poses work in time with your breath. Begin each pose by taking a deep breath in and then breath out while you complete that pose. When you move on to the next pose take another deep breath in and out.

Meditating on phrases and mantras

Begin by generating a motivational thought or phrase for the meditation session. Recite the phrase softly to yourself a number of times. Consider the general meaning of the phrase. Then consider how the phrase relates to your experiences.

You can also meditate on a mantra, which is a sound or a few words that you repeat to yourself either silently or out loud. Mantras are useful to shut out distractions from the outside world, as you can focus solely on the sound. Some of the most commonly used mantras are listed below, but you can write down your own mantra and repeat it to yourself if there is a phrase or word that is meaningful to you.

Mantra	Meaning or origin
The Om or Aum	It is, will be or to become
Om Namah Shivaya	I bow to Shiva
Hare Krishna Hare Krishna, Krishna Krishna Hare Hare, Hare Rama Hare Rama, Rama Rama, Hare Hare	Hare Krishna is a branch of Hinduism
I am that I am for his name	The answer God gave to Moses when asked
Aham-Prema	I am divine love
Om Mani Padme Hum	Hail the jewel in the lotus

Affirmations

Affirmations can also be very effective when used as topics of contemplation throughout the day. This is true for any of the teachings we may read or hear, including the information in this book. The knowledge is really of no use unless we put it into action.

You could choose one topic per day for meditation and contemplation. Meditate on the topic at home and then take the topic with you, contemplating it in differing circumstances: driving, on the train or bus, at work, dealing with people, shopping or having coffee with a friend.

Ask yourself, 'How does the topic relate to the situation I am in now? How could it help me deal with this situation, this person, this emotion?'

By relating a chosen affirmation to your own life, circumstances and experiences, it can become very effective in changing your thoughts and actions. If we don't meditate on or contemplate them in this way they are nothing more than nice sounding words.

Five positive affirmations:

1. I have everything I need right now for an abundant life.
2. Kindness is free.
3. I am strong.
4. I am powerful.
5. All I need is within me right now.

66

Learn to enjoy the way as
much as you would enjoy when
you reach the destination.

99

Sakshi Chetana

After your meditation

When you have finished your meditation, take a moment to think about how it made you feel and how you would like to take those thoughts and feelings with you as you go through the rest of the day. Don't rush to get back to whatever task is pulling you away or you may lose the positive benefits gained from taking the time to slow down in the first place.

A good practice is to keep a meditation journal where you can keep track of your progress so far. Make a space to write down how you feel after your meditation. Do you feel relaxed and peaceful or restless and self-critical because you weren't able to remain in the moment for as long as you would have liked? How long did you meditate for? What thoughts arose as you were meditating? Were you able to remain mindful throughout?

Remember, your journal should not be a place to be too negative. If something didn't work out as you had planned, take a note of it and see it as a step in your journey. We all have days when things don't go as planned; this is normal. Be kind to yourself and above all try to keep a regular meditation practice. If you can make it a part of your daily routine, you will reap the rewards in the rest of your life.